SITTING IN SILENCE

Poetry & Prose

by

NICHOLAS RINTH

This book is a work of fiction. Names, characters, businesses, places, events, and incidents either are the product of the author's imagination or are used fictitiously. Any resemblance to actual persons, living or dead, events or locales is entirely coincidental.

Copyright © 2017 by Nicholas Rinth. All rights reserved.

No part of this publication may be reproduced, distributed, or transmitted in any form or by any means, including photocopying, recording, or other electronic or mechanical methods, without the prior written permission of the author, except in the case of brief quotations embodied in book reviews and certain other noncommercial uses permitted by copyright law.

Thank you for your support of the author's rights.

Author website: www.nrinth.wordpress.com
Contact information: nicholasrinth@gmail.com

ISBN: 978-0-9988216-8-9 (Print)

PRINTED IN THE UNITED STATES OF AMERICA
FIRST EDITION

To Thomas,

*for making my life
brighter and more bearable
since our meeting.*

CONTENT

Author's Note.................................. 09

Part I: Reminisce............................ 15

Part II: Relapse.............................. 57

Part III: Realization........................ 95

Part IV: Recovery........................... 123

I want to walk in that howling wind
'til it scatters all my thoughts.
Sit all alone on that riverbank
'til I forget that I can talk.
Just listen.

– Conor Oberst, *Time Forgot*

AUTHOR'S NOTE

Sitting in Silence is a compilation of letters, scrawls, and free verse poems that I've written throughout the years.

It's the product of a mood that has a tendency of checking in on me during the most absurd of times. Though it isn't a physical thing, I liken the mood to an animal. The cruel, parasitic sort. Since it appears when it's hungry and goes when it's satisfied—whether that takes months or a scant few days is never certain. But I remember it haunting the best and worst periods of my life, and it just so happens that this year, the contents of this book was the outcome. Don't be mistaken in believing that this is a creature of inspiration, however, because it isn't.

Far from it, in fact.

This beast is an encompassing thing that serves only itself. Prolonged contact may worsen perspectives, cripple dignity, and permanently affect the mind. I know these feelings well, and I've tried to detail some of their more... bitter flavors here, while interspersing a few of my own banal struggles of love and life in between.

Many of my words in the coming pages will always linger in the back of my head, but I'm proud to say that most, I've already gotten past. While time's attention shatters everyone, age still holds a number of benefits—experience being on the top of that list, followed closely by the license to act like an all-knowing sage. There's something about wrinkles deep enough to shelve books that screams wisdom to people.

Yearly accolades aside, I'm proud to say that my record for getting through bad days is perfect, if not a little wrecked on some pages. Still, whenever I read my old letters... it's nostalgic—how empty I felt then.

Let it be known that the letters I've chosen to include here were all written throughout different periods of my life and some have months, even years, spanning between them, so I'm not necessarily talking about the same occasion... but I'm rambling now, speaking of things that don't matter both to you, and to this book. Just know that these words have all been felt at one time or another, and honestly, I don't remember the exact instances of their feeling, but that doesn't change the truth they hold or what they once meant to me.

I've always liked to think of myself an expert at forgetting things, so that's what I've become.

If some of my words unwittingly cause nostalgia or light a few flames within you however, then as an author, there's nothing more I could ask for. Fantasy stories have always been a love of mine, and I've found incomparable enjoyment in writing my characters and developing them into something that others can read and relate to, but to be able to touch the hearts of people through my own firsthand experiences, well, that's indescribable.

Again, I'm rambling.

Truthfully, I have so much more to say, so much more nonsense to impart, but this is getting long now. Unbearably so. And I do have a schedule to keep—neither do I want to keep you from your own. So, to end this, allow me to thank you for buying this book. It means a great deal to me. Much, much more than you could ever know.

I hope you enjoy the small journey I've prepared for you.

Warmest Regards,

Nicholas Rinth

Angels bring you home.

I feel like I don't belong here now, but my ruined tongue doesn't know the way back home.

PART I

Reminisce

*"Lost in a world between
dream and awake."*

How is it that a simple scent can make me feel as though my whole world is going to crash down on my shoulders?

Like I can't breathe, and I have to hunker down with my head buried between my knees because I can't let anymore pieces of myself go. I'm already missing so many.

So, so many.

Adrift

I wonder how it feels for a tamed bird to rush
through the skies, and settle upon a perch
that so wholly offers safety and a home.

Rest, Friend

The air breaks. His vision blurs.
The world sharpens, then splits
from edge to edge until—
she speaks.
And the crash back into himself
is violent, but grounding.
Because he knows now.
This is a dream.
A deluded fantasy conjured from
too much to drink.
Pooled longing for someone
trapped behind wood and nails.
Six feet out of reach.

Things Denied

I long to wake in the circle of your arms. Safe and warm and uncaring for the torpid passage of time.

I Need Some Sleep

Racking up memories only to be caught in that age long moment when nostalgia ruins more than I thought possible.

Heat

We speak, as if that might change things.

But our words have never been worth anything in the wild, white blaze of pent-up rage.

SEARCHING

The skies are crying tonight,
Their tears force the world to shine,
Dripping down, silent, with the promise of better days,
They don't wash things away,

The sidewalk's a jeweler in the rain,
Filled with gum drops and fake, glinting stains,
So, I pocket both hands and trail the sad, yellow paint,
It doesn't show me the way,

My head's been a mess for so long,
I look up and wonder if I should go on,
But the lights that come toward me trap me in place,
They don't let me walk away,

I'm tumbling on the road again,
The present's got me tangled in my own skin,
There's people screaming, panicked, yet steady gazed,
They all look my way,

What should I do now?
I'm so tired, I can't figure it out,
But after so long, there's one thing I've learned—
The world will continue to turn.

When Words Are Born

The words in my throat keep bending,
And I'm so tired of trying to speak.
I feel like I'm going to waste a lot of ink tonight.

To Try and To Fail

We speak, yet say nothing.
Still, the question remains,
Dancing on the tip of my tongue,
Lingering in the air like toxic paint,
"Why wasn't I enough?"

Clutch

That day when I held your hands tightly,
was I really able to hold onto our happiness?

Rain

Delirious, heat filled rain.

The sky's jewels,

Dripping like melted silver,

And farmer's salvation,

Forcing cobble paths to glint,

Old rocks to shine,

Molding nature into a world—

more beautiful, less creased.

The tears of an unseen Mother,

That weeps in the hopes

to wash all of the bad things away.

Almost human,

Yet, still, more than most.

Whisper to me in that tone for which I pine...

Happy.
It's not as perfect as when you were with me.

Beyond my Fingertips

You're that word on the tip of my tongue. That perfect fit. The one I know would be just right. The one that can make it all seem better. The one I try so damn hard for.

The one always out of my reach.

Unrequited

"It's over now," the voices in my head say,

repeating words that fade like paper in the rain.

I never listen—of course I don't—my ears are deaf.

Tuned only to a voice that doesn't feel the same.

A city of life and splendor, of wonders and riches—filled with people blurring past, all too lost in the moment, slaves working for a better future; or so they tell themselves.

And here I sit, bereft, as I look at the echoes of my past in the form of chipped paint, old cars, and black gumdrop stains, with the realization that soon, even these will be gone from me.

Life's too fast. My legs can't keep up anymore, so here, I'll stop, here, I'll rest... observing, waiting, hoping for someone to cross that eight-step street and reminisce with me of a time when jukeboxes still sang and telephones could spin—*please.*

I could use a friend.

One that understands.

One that remembers.

Gone

The sun shines light over the haze,

tearing me away from the dark,

and the shadow of my friend,

who I can't will back to this plane.

Macabre

It's red.
The rolling shards of glass
crunched under my hands.
Aged twenty porcelain
torn in twos and fours and tens.
Priced ink shattered at the seams.
Koi's bleed, giving flowers life.
Not so permanent after all.
Numbness spreads, disconnecting.
But all I see, all that matters is—
it's red.

OPEN LETTER #13

Dear —,

I miss you.

And I know that that's so incredibly selfish of me, but I just can't help it. I miss you. I miss you. I miss you. I can go on and on all day about anything and everything so long as I'm with you, but those three words are like a mantra in my mind repeating over and over. A phrase of personal torture. And you know what's really scary? I can't make it stop.

My memories of you have a mind of their own. A little monster with beady eyes and sharp teeth, banging on the walls of my subconscious, cracking it, crawling through, and I'm just so sick of it. I want it to stop. God, do I want it to stop. Because I actually kind of like it—and I hate that. Hate that I love waking up to the thought of you. Of your grin, of our shared interests, of our playful disagreements, of our not so distant memories. I swear that I can still hear you calling out to me. Still hear your reactions by my side whenever I find something stupid that I could only send to you.

But that's all these are: thoughts of you.

And it's so hard trying to experience something when all I can do is wish you were here to experience it, too. So, please, I beg of you, leave my mind because I'm not strong enough to let go on my own. Cut the cord. I love our friendship, but having to kill my feelings with you right there is too hard to endure, and I'm afraid that if this goes on, then I might end up resenting you. I don't want that. Good god, please anything but that.

I miss you, and this distance is fucking painful but when you're speaking to me all the time and talking to me like I'm someone important, I can't stop missing you. Please let go or please speak up. I'm tired of these mixed signals and these mindless games because I'm already madly, furiously in love with you—haven't I made that obvious enough?

Delusions

Wasting words on the world like we know it, while leaving the ones that need to be uttered in the air; I wasn't trying to avoid them. I just thought that we had a silent promise. Some mutual understanding of sorts.

A secret only between us—in the form of unspoken affection that would blossom when ready.

How stupid I felt during that frigid morning when I realized that I allowed my fantasies to get the better of me.

Power

When the world is still and silence lingers, I wonder if you think of me, if I even grace your thoughts.

I envy the ones that do. Because your attention has the power to make or break my day.

I hate that.

Lament

Haunted by the memories of years past,
The signs of the future are lost to yesterday,
Where the part of me that dwells in unforgotten silence,
Drowns in the uncompromising waves
Of what could've been.

Echoes

Drowning in my head,
With these revolving daydreams
And never ending scrawls
Cutting reminders of spun dreams,
Of another place, another time,
Another me.

REGRET

That rainy afternoon,
When I caught your wrist,
Locking it between a stubborn grip,
You stopped,
and for one, endless moment,
You didn't pull away.
Brown clashed with brown.
No longer able to blend,
yet I could still see it—
still feel it.
The wasted love that remained.
Unspoken words, defiant tilts,
Old, familiar hands,
A wash of warmth my angry chest
couldn't handle.
So sudden and so fierce,
my jaw slackened against my will.
My grip eased, and then—
you turned away.
Escaping through the plain wooden door,
painted a cheerful cream,
encasing me in silence.
Thick and oppressive.

Distress

I can't run to you now,
and that kills me,
more than you can fathom.
Because I've always considered myself
on the list of those that will.

Restless

Tossing, turning, and tossing again.
But when I wake,
The nightmares escape.
Oh, I'm grateful for that.

Television Blues

You left,

but we're both to blame.

Now, I must sit here with the remains,

of an old box with blown-out speakers.

Artificial laughter in the form of

actors and actresses, scripted to feel.

They radiate white noise and strange blurs.

My own horde of false company

in empty space.

I once thought that you couldn't mourn something that was never yours.
As it turns out, yes...
Yes you can.

It was all in my head.
I should've known.
The best things are.

I miss myself sometimes.
The version that loved you.
He seemed much kinder.

The lonely spot in my mind where the thought of us dwells is especially mocking today.

Nightly

I remain here, swaddled in silence,
Noise spinning in my head,
Trying to command my pen—ha!
As if it's ever obeyed me before.
These buried scrawls and conjured fantasies,
Are but proof that time passes strangely in the dark,
Moments collect by the handful,
Seconds pile into minutes,
And minutes into nothing at all,
Until all that's left are harsh truths,
That my unlit soul can't take.

SCRAWLS

I can utter words that smooth out the edges of my friend's souls, while I sit here, pretending like command the jagged thorns around my own.

Some scars are long and deep and veiled by life. They ruin me during the nights when the world is as quiet as the day you left.

Have you ever told someone you loved them and all they do is make this awful face? A mix between cross, confusion, and pity. Like they don't want to deal with it.

Oh, but I never wanted to deal with it either.

Your caring hands and lingering touches have always made me light up in ways I thought existed only in heaven and in dreams.

I closed my eyes, expecting hurt. Fresh and biting. Yet when the seconds ticked on and it never came, I wonder why those moments of frightful expectation were more agonizing than the pain itself.

OPEN LETTER #20

Dear—,

It's raining outside—or I believe it is. I've got the music turned up and really, who can hear anything when that smooth voice of your favorite musician reaches out through time and space just to caress your ears?

But as I'm sitting here at my desk, lost in yesterday, an invisible vocalist my only companion, I can't help but take a peek at the world outside.

As it turns out, it isn't raining.

I must be imagining things then. (Again.) It certainly wouldn't surprise me. It's been happening quite a lot lately, perhaps it's a symptom of bereavement. I wouldn't know, nor am I in the mood to ponder. Because all I can think about right now is that ghost lingering in the form of your scent and dry laughter, wondering if it'll leave me alone tonight.

Letting go is never easy, especially when all that's left is a gray stone to talk to.

You're not here anymore. I know that.

I don't need the reminder.

Haiku Stack

Here, I sit, bereft,
Listening for lost voices,
In dingy car lots,

Remnants of a time,
When I could still call your name,
And pray mine followed,

Life was better then,
When we were young and too bold,
When you called me yours.

Only

glare acidic enough to scald,
chin tilted in defiance,
and mouth curved down
into a stubborn grimace.
still, I wish for no one...
besides you,
and this ten-bob intimacy,
much more shocking and urgent
than all the rest.

Where Did It All Go Wrong?

Premature wrinkles over furrowed brows
are a testament of my old regrets,
and even older grievances.

They're the echoes of a time
when the world was flipped on its side
and all of the roads stretched out before me
led only to awful choices.

Some of the turns I made were light and swift,
done without much thought,
while the rest brought rivers of tears down my cheeks,
salty stings that are only good for softening
the harshness of the rest of the world.

Regardless, each decision still lingers
like unshakable sand in the back of my head,
making time pass strangely when I'm alone
in the shadow of my own darkness.

Caught

To see you angry hurts,

but to see you tongue-tied,

fumbling for an explanation

you don't know how to give,

and stuttering your way through

with broken words and brittle convictions

is decidedly worse.

Diversions

Lightheaded with heat,

Air siphoned from lungs,

Absent, wandering attention,

Focus shifting to foreboding distances,

Dappling light and elusive stars,

Busy bees for eyes,

Brain kept occupied with thoughts—

Of green stems, Cobble paths, and red tiled rooftops,

Of dirty shoes, angry cars, and gleaming puddles.

Filled and far,

Far away from you.

Evening Cigarette

Windows starred with deathly fog,
Glass droplets falling from the sky,
Pooling around my world,
Rivulets of false, glinting paint,
And weeping lullabies.

Worlds Apart

Words uttered without conviction,

Lost to time and chance,

Memories twisted to suit weakness,

Endless tomorrow's,

A cacophony of—

Drowsy days and ghastly nights,

All I hear are bottles...

clinking in my head,

rampant and overflowing.

I don't want sleep,

I desire rest.

Move Along

I hate the knowledge that I can go on without you. How I can just trudge along and carry through the days given enough time; how it'll be easier after a few more torpid months.

I don't want it to reach that.

I just want you.

... Is that so hard to understand?

Warm Flashes

A day without melodies and deafening silence,

Reminds me of the ghosts of my past.

Quick to offer love.

Quicker to pull it away.

PERFECT ILLUSION

Time and talk and chances missed,
Splayed locks and a lingering kiss,
I can hear them, you know—those risks, cold and dead,
Filled with thoughts and feelings left unsaid,

They taste of memories and ink,
Of days gone to waste in just one blink,
Ghosts haunting me, cold and piercing,
Smiling passionately, painful and much too fleeting,

I miss that smile on my face,
When you were there to make my heart race,
I dream of your callousness wrapped before affection,
Of your flawed hands—my absolute perfection,

But as the days grow cold and winter blooms,
Even my fantasies grow tired, and I'm sure my regret will, too,
My mind will soon be overburdened and heavy,
My lips frozen cold, still unable to speak with liberty,

Because I'm a coward when my heart's at stake,
Self-mute, stubborn, and always a little too late,
That's why I sit here with my memories, idle and blue,
Lost in yesterday, where I'm still with you.

Withering leaves and rotting things shame me with their honesty.

Smile fade.
Happiness, too.
And even pain.
So, I wonder when our memories will as well.
I'm tired of missing you.

PART II

Relapse

*"It's not that I want to die,
I just don't particularly want to live either."*

Time creeps when pain is fresh, extending life into something a little less bearable. But when the sting wears off, time begins to run again. Quiet and unnoticed.

We hardly think of how long those nights had been or the amount of tears we wasted. Not until those hands grind to a halt once more, and we're left staring at nothing with an aching chest and the thought of tomorrow.

I knew then that time hated us all.

Quite equally.

OPEN LETTER #9

Dear —,

There are some days when I feel good about life, about the world. But more often than not, on days like today, I just can't find the strength to get up anymore. I hardly see any reason to. And that one song playing on repeat certainly isn't helping matters. But I feel as though I'm not going anywhere, and I just want to do what I want, but of course I can't. Reality's a bitch that comes knocking. Always.

And since the paper won't judge me, I'll say now that I'm scared. I don't believe in my own capabilities because time and time again, I can see just how mediocre they are. And it's easier to hide out in this stupid room of mine, hating myself. A million others do it. Blending seems to be a shared talent of ours. I wonder if I'll continue to be swept away by this pace or if I'll break it—I wonder how to even begin.

Well, I don't suppose it really matters. I'll end up dead either way. One of the choices is just a bit faster than the other.

(Perhaps less painful, too.)

Alone

Red-nosed and seated on the grass,
Broken by the echoes of ages past,
Winter's expanse has come and brought the gray,
Somehow, I'm glad that you got away,
Because your stone replacement can't suffer the cold,
But now I must shiver here, on my own.

Intimacy

One look, and I'm lost.
One hug, and I'm grounded.
One arduous whisper, and my knees
are gone beneath me.
It isn't the lack of control I fear.
It's this...
Tenderness. Intimacy. Affection.
Things too hot to touch.
I fear my own vulnerability.
And I pray you don't take advantage.

Flimsy

Her feelings are bared in her eyes.
But after so long, it hurts.
Made worse with the tentative care
in each uncertain caress.
Made agonizing with every apology
I cannot accept.
There's no need. There never has been.
Any mistake she thinks she's made
has been accepted, understood, and
forgiven long ago.
Because I'm a glutton for punishment.
Weak and sick to death
of my own heart.

Nerves

She whispers his name,
and it fills the room from
floor to ceiling,
drowning him in softness.
The dense, unfathomable emptiness
that once enveloped him
is suddenly pierced
by the sound of falling rocks.
Loud drums that echo
in his ears—
'*His heart*,' he realizes
a second too late.
Beating blood, working muscle,
running off like a flock
of startled birds.

OPEN LETTER #19

Dear —,

I can physically feel monotony.

The way it settles, abrupt, coming from nowhere and always surprising. I try to change my routine, only to find myself staring numbly as the world passes me by. I go out, only to talk to no one and smile awkwardly at the sales people asking how I am. Do I look okay? If I do, then I'm glad. It was difficult to leave the house today.

The noises in my head are too loud to be drowned out by anything except that one song I can't seem to stop listening to. Uplifting it may be, but it only drags me deeper into this hole I call my own. Where dullness and misery are my best—and only—companions.

During the worst of these times, when I'm sitting before my dingy computer screen with a cup of coffee and too much to do, but not enough motivation to do… any of it, I wish life would ~~end~~ begin again. I want to breathe, I miss the feeling of doing so. I miss the feeling of contentment, of satisfaction, of ease… of home.

It's cold. So, so cold.

But the heater's on and it's sunny outside, so I can only suppose that it must be my imagination playing tricks on me again. A very palpable trick. My blankets too far away though—two steps too far. Just out of reach. I wish I could stretch and never have to leave this room. I wish time would stand still for a day and just let me catch up with the rest of the world.

I have one more wish. A bit less selfish than the rest. Simpler, too. Once you receive this, please tell me everything's alright.

I know it is, but… I could really stand to hear it.

Final Flickers

Imagine a flickering candle drowning itself
in wax that once kept it aloft.
Swift and slow all at once.
A moment that lasts an age and a lifetime.
That's what hope dying looks like.

On the Brain

I think of you.
You, and little else.
How much more
would you ask of me?

Incubus

His laughter gives her visions
of melted chocolate and honey.
Rich and too warm to hold.
Pools of darkness swirl,
curling at the pit of her stomach,
forcing her to reach out.
And the fear of burning herself no longer matters.
The only thing of any import now is his voice—
And that he never stop speaking.

A slave to this future that I need.

Tumbling down again.
When will I
be allowed rest?
I'm tired of standing.

Boat Master

Sliding to my knees, unable to entertain the thought of letting go. How can I? When you're a welcome dock—proud and sturdy against the volatile waves.

And I'm a broken ship, barely able to moor after suffering another endless journey.

Please don't turn me away.

Half-awake

And I fear the day when I wake, looking beside me with a smile in my eyes and good morning on my lips, only to realize that I've been dreaming too long. Because the bed is cold. The mirror's reflection is my only companion.

And no matter how hard I try, I can't go back to sleep.

SCRAWLS

> How faithless of my mind to forget me in grief,
> yet somehow leave every line of your face intact.

I'll be by your side until you can look at me
with happiness in your eyes
that rivals the you I didn't get
the chance to love.

> My final thought before bed
> and the first in the still morning
> has been the same since meeting you.

It's so hard trying to experience something
when all I can do is with you
were here to experience it, too.

SCRAWLS

This fragile heart of mine is too full. It's going to wreck and tangle the casual strings of our attachment.

I hope you don't turn away.

Not again.

> You keep making sense of all these twisted things and then turning away. But I don't need you to fix my world.
>
> Just stay in it a while longer.

I have a lot of love to give. More than any one person knows what to do with. And so, on the bad days, I sit and wait in fear for you to return it to me. Sick and tired.

Oh, so tired.

I'm sorry.

Tired

How can you just forgive everything I've done?
When here I am, feeling like I profane
the very ground I walk upon.
Is it really that easy to fall asleep?
Because I've been sitting here,
angry and waiting to remember
how to adore my own seams.

Breathe

Livid and exhausted when the sun sets.
All that's left to do now is rest.
When morning comes, I'll look up at the rays.
See if I'm willing to give myself a few more days.

1,000 PAPER CRANES

I folded a crane
Hoping for something
That always eluded me

I made it a companion
For it seemed lonely
On its own atop my shelf

Then I folded ten more
I got a paper cut
Copper stained one wing

Soon, I had a hundred
And I waited for the day
They'd all add up

506, 507, 508, 509
789, 790, 791
So close

888, 889
A little more
997, 998, 999

My hope swelled
My fantasies grew
I was surprisingly happy

Then I reached a thousand
I screamed the news
My expectations skyrocketed

I tried so hard
I boldly declared my convictions
My wish? Isn't it obvious?

I didn't get it
And I'm sleepless now
Though it's my fault

I folded cranes
Thinking. Dreaming, Hoping
That what we had would clear

I forgot to ask your wants
Assuming, not expecting that—
You had none.

Feel a Fool

During the early hours of dawn, when I wait for my memories to come out and play, I realized that some ghosts could be summoned.

I like to think that it was my desire to avoid them that caused me to reach for your shoulders, scrambling for purchase long gone, searching for warmth in a place I've already been told I have no home, but that would be a lie.

I know my reasons best.

I've always been a simple man—and defeat has never tasted so good than against your lips.

Immersion

There's something about the way she said my name.
Groggy, breathless, and entirely too drawn out.
It made me feel as though everyone had been
saying it wrong my entire life.

OPEN LETTER #23

Dear—,

During particularly cold days, when 12AM rolls around, I sit down, heart hurting and limbs heavy, exhaustion from the world trailing after me, dragging me a little deeper in my seat. And I wonder what everyone else is doing and who they're with. Which ones feel the same and which ones are fortunate enough to call themselves… well, not happy exactly, but content. It seems like such an impossible thing. Far-off and too gargantuan too grasp. Yet for some it's right there, existing within sight.

Perhaps it once did for me as well.

No, I'm certain it did.

But now, in my solitude, I'm sporting a noisy head and shitty lenses, blackening my outlook. A testament to my fall from favor. Honestly, I'd rather have a black eye. At least that would give me something physical to focus on. Something I could use as an excuse to properly take care of myself.

Perhaps, one day, I'll be lucky enough to wake up and find satisfaction sitting next to me, bright and smiling blindly, but until then, I suppose I'll have to get up and search for it on my own. In people, in food, in coffee and writing and cats.

Because 12AM's about to pass again.

The time for thinking's done. I need to go to sleep. The sun will rise soon, and that blasted thing waits for no one. I'll sleep soundly knowing you'll be gone when I wake, though I hope tomorrow's silence is a little more forgiving.

Comforting, too, so long as you're still listening.

Until then, good night.

SCRAWLS

> Alcohol saved for a special occasion.
> Well, I'm feeling special now.

My composure cracks,
and then it shatters,
revealing talent and insanity,
as banal as the rest of me.

> So, here we are again.
> Like you never left.
> I'm so weak.

Secrets never ending, so as not to lay bare,
The humor you'd find in my life of regret.

> You left so quickly.
> How can I not worry?
> I hope you remember to stay warm.

Despair doesn't kill, just makes life a little more unbearable.

My mind's a battleground.

OFTEN OVERLOOKED

It scares me to know that I can write pages upon pages of one little action of yours.

I'm completely at your mercy—overthinking and questioning absolutely everything—and you have no idea. I'm scared to know what would happen if you did.

Is my heart safe in your keeping?

Can you handle it? Care for it?

From the recent rollercoaster of emotions I've been going through, I'd say you don't quite know what to do with the thing. Though I can't exactly blame you... because I don't either.

Perhaps that's why I so readily offered it to you.

How goddamn foolish of me.

ENSNARE

The shackles have gone now, the fetters removed,
Detached from reality, twice, I claw at these leftover maroons
Marks long gone, yet still burn red,
They itch—these monstrous things—they hurt, they ache,
They snarl in the dead of night when I alone remain,

My lips speak freedom, my soul cries life,
But my wrists have only known the whispers of strife,
My shoulders droop, overburdened and heavy,
Still I cry out, because the promise of liberty,
Is too wonderful to live without,

It's right there, as it has always been,
Just beyond reach, perfect little illusion,
It drives me mad and pushes me to the brink,
Mocks me with images that please everything,
Yet, at once, this keeps me sane—somehow,

And I don't know what or who to believe in anymore,
Certainly not me; because when I look the shackles are gone,
Their scratches were delusions, their pain was just the same,
My eyes are open and the world is clear—I can see!
My light is shining, it's calling out to me,

Yet when I reach out, I swear those monstrous things move,

Those imaginary grips tighten,

and they murmur their unintelligible lies,

So soft, far too sweet—they reel me back

into the comforts of their terribly tight embrace,

Where I'm trapped again,

wondering why I should leave where I belong.

Bad Aftertaste

Defeat. Rejection. Doubt. Betrayal.

Swallowing words. Vile thoughts. Cutting laughter.

Cruel friends. Lost family.

Self-hate.

Languid Morning

It's gray out, but there's no rain.

My coffee's gone stale.

Worse than the cigarette haze on my tongue.

At my desk, life seems faraway.

Distant, here in my lethargic bubble,

Penetrated only by—

Dust showers,

Lua's playing in the background.

Sounding out against the calm,

A broken voice, beautiful in the infant dawn,

And, you—

Well…

The sun wakes.

OPEN LETTER #35

Dear—,

I hate my recurring thoughts.

They speak of truths that I'm already familiar with, of instances in my head that I once twisted to suit my own weaknesses, of past problems that I don't need bogging me down...

I already have too many of those. Too many.

I don't need reminders of the days when it hurt to be alive because there they are, always lingering one step behind, prepared to pounce on me should I unwittingly open that door. Hell, sometimes I'm not even near it, sometimes I'm just sitting down utterly bored or way too happy and the thing flies right open. As if forced to by a gale of cruelty that I don't understand, but I know one thing... it has this tendency of following me around. Of vanishing and returning at the strangest of times.

I'm not dense enough to not realize what that cutting wind might be, neither do I seek help for it.

It's there, and that's that.

I know the draft will pass, and though they may turn into full blown hurricanes, even those lose their potency in the face of the unyielding sea.

I have never once needed help with compartmentalizing all of the thoughts that run rampant inside of my mind.

I suppose, what I'm really trying to say is that...

Today, I'm just tired of feeling tired.

Embrace

The wind is cold. There's no sun.

Outside, the air's heavy and stale.

Even clouds get tired of crying some days.

Like the reflection I see

on my tar cellphone screen.

An echo of myself,

swaddled on this rumpled bed.

Tendrils of smoke drifting round.

Eyes groggy, limbs protesting.

Thoughts muffled by ocean waves.

Drowned out by numbness.

Long and lasting.

Migraine

Voices echo against the stillness around me, but I hardly notice. They're no more than scarce whispers, hushes lullabies when compared to the constant ringing in my head. In my ears.

Blinding flashes akin to sudden shouts that make the back of my eyes protest until they're forced to close. It's reflex. And as I sit there, waiting for the dizziness to subside and sound to return, I realize that…

It's nice to have a reason other than terror to shut my eyes.

Blues

They say the sun changes things.

Turns the night's perspectives into something a little saner. But I no longer remember how long I've stood here—used, tired, a lonely sentinel left to wait for the warmth of something I've already lost to wash over me.

Bogged down by smiles caught in yesterday.

So many relationships are both burnt and lost to the heat of the moment. Self-control is also a virtue.

PART III

Realization

"I'll tell you a secret:
There's peace in caring for yourself."

Memories are such cruel and stabbing things.

They're good for a time, but just when life gets a little rough, they have no qualms about haunting you, making you feel inexplicably lonely, gifting you with sadness beyond reason—and what then? What happens after?

You fall into a downward spiral into the past where grief lingers and the flickers of someone that was once you dwells, mocking. Then you realize their burden.

And, once again, you're left searching for light.

Burning

Drunk with emotion.

Like the hazy dreams of illness once you finally wake. Except this is more memorable. This is joyful and here and true.

This is what it means to succumb to the overwhelming relief of having you so close to me that there's hardly even space for breath between us.

Lingering

She pauses here and there without reason, drawing in a breath before grinning into his mouth. And the delight he feels then is a physical thing. Too soft and too tender for him to touch.

Not yet.

His hands are still rough. His self-esteem, cutting. He isn't ready. This is good as it is.

It also isn't enough.

No More

I care for you more delicately than I do my pen. I consider your voice over the hundreds vying in my mind. I reached out to you with hope I believed long dead… but no more.

Because this has become a game now, and I'm so tired of twisted things.

I forfeit.

Accountability

I can so easily recall days when we'd run off to steal a few moments to ourselves. When we forgot about the world together. But my emotions have always been intense things. Some more than most can handle.

I never thought they'd be too much. In hindsight, I probably should've known. I got careless.

My fault. Not yours.

OPEN LETTER #25

Dear—,

My feelings for you are fading.

I noticed when I was no longer hanging on your every word, when I could go for days without talking to you and not worrying or even noticing that I hadn't. And that makes me truly happy. It's what I've wanted for so long, after having all of these tiresome circles to run around. But—yes, there is always that one, horrid contradiction—I can't help the wash of disappointment I feel whenever we do speak. Because there was something there. Unspeakable and lingering, a quiet comfort of sorts. And I know in my gut that there was potential for greatness between us.

But it's gone now. Almost.

Did you feel it, too? If so, will you regret it? I certainly will.

"Life's too short for regrets," people say.

'Foolishness,' I think.

And because I'm a glutton for punishment I believe in making as many regrets as you possibly can. Life is built upon them. Because only then do you know the inadequacies of your own self... and then grow. Learn from the missed chances and the cowardice and the stupidity. But, this is a discussion for another time, perhaps between you and I, during a night spent drinking on lonely rooftops and cursing at stars.

Yes, I will thoroughly regret the cracked glass that is now us. It's irreparable, really, but that's okay. I don't particularly want to fix it. It's the scar left from me being exactly who I was, and not being enough for you. I wasn't enough to evoke the needed emotion to spring you into action, neither was I able to coax anything more than vague replies and ambiguous grins. The effort wasn't wasted, however, and I hold no ill feelings. I'm not what you wanted—and that's perfectly okay. I'm glad we were still able to maintain a relationship, even if it isn't the sort I initially wanted.

It's still fun in an awful, bittersweet way. The sparks are gone now. Well, almost. They're already out the door at least, lingering by the front mat and glimpsing back a few more times to extend the hurt for as long as they possibly can. Blasted things. But I've been in this position enough times to know that in their place will be the deep settlement of understanding and passing twinges of grief.

And yet, I'm happy for it all the same.

Because that's familiar territory. Easy to tread, easier to live through.

I know I can handle it.

Shoulder

I'll accept this hardship with my own two hands, despite their tired calluses because it's what you bring with you.

And I would have you no other way.

50 Words

The cicadas scream today.
Loud. Vibrant.
No longer submerged by the pitter patter
of heavy rain.
The sun shines—and here I remain.
Still.
By my window.
Coffee in hand.
Waiting for the world to wake.
Footsteps amble to my side.
She speaks,
And my legs are gone beneath me.

Tin

I thought I'd steeled my heart.
Thought that I'd crafted the perfect
Iron wrap to shield myself with.
But...
You smile when you look at me,
And that's never happened before.

I FEEL GOOD TODAY

Look at them.

Those concrete squares filled with different people. Young and old. Experienced and not. They move about their lives, unaware, and perhaps even uncaring for the rest that linger beside them.

Worlds are created in those apartments, they're brought up, ever so slowly. Some are turned into places that could be called home, while others are mere cases for the rolling stones within—and me... well, here I stand, I stare, and I look up at the starless sky drowned out by electronic lights. I listen to the silence drowned out by incoherent noise, and I bask in it all.

No one notices me here, nor do I want to be seen.

This is my world, and here, I don't much care about them either.

Don't abandon what you can't replace.

You can't escape what you don't want to.

Well, as long as you're happy, I don't really care what happens.

Ticking

You slipped through my fingers
like the fading edges of a dream.
So important at the time of waking,
but come midday,
the clock has had its way
with my thoughts.
And my emotions.

OPEN LETTER #8

Dear —,

Aren't you tired of these games?

It's 4AM, and I'm sitting here, waiting for one of us to admit... something. Because god, if I'm not tired. To hell with mixed signals and guessing games. As if matters of the heart aren't complicated enough.

I've been clear with my wants, it's you I can't read. One minute I can see our future together, and the next I can see it crumbling. I just can't do this anymore. I'm sorry—I don't even know why I am. Maybe it's because I thought there was some potential in us. If only I had enough balls to risk it, if only you'd been a little clearer. Of maybe you were, and like a fool that read too much into meaningless actions, I ignored the signs that you weren't interested. Maybe that's why you never went after me. But if you were interested and were just waiting for me to say something, then I really am sorry for my own incompetence to speak up. I couldn't read you—and that's not your fault, nor am I blaming you—I was just afraid I'd scare you away, ruin our friendship with talks of ardor, ruin the memories of the nights we spent out 'til dawn talking about every little nothing that came to mind.

I'm digressing, aren't I? That seems to be happening a lot lately… whenever you're the subject. Again, I'm sorry. What I truly wanted to say was that I'm tired. I don't want to interpret the meaning behind your actions—if they had any at all. I don't want to play anymore. I'm going to back off. Wholly. Entirely. Completely. I'll step away. I'll change my tone into something purely platonic, and I'm sorry if I bothered you with my feelings. I didn't mean to. I give up. Call me a coward. It's okay. I am.

I'll miss this. I'll miss the thought of us. But I'm just so tired right now. I don't want to let life pass me by because I'm too busy hung up over you. I'm going to move forward. Now. After this letter. If you want to take that step with me, then that's entirely up to you. I'd welcome you. Always. Just know that I'm going ahead regardless of your decision.

Still, a part of me hopes you'll follow. If you don't, however, I'll understand. It's just another feeling to crush. And I'll look forward to the day that these passions are nothing more than echoes, but when they are, I hope you don't come after me wanting anything more than friendship because I never want to hurt you.

I never want to break your heart the way I did my own.

SCRAWLS

You keep speaking of the past,
As if you were any different then.

> When we're together,
> things become undefinable.
> I loved that—once.
> Now, I'm only tired of it.

Don't worry.
Pain is temporary,
as all things seem to be.
And that's just the problem isn't it?

> The path towards you is unforgiving.
> Oh, but the path away is so much worse.

SCRAWLS

> Things can change when what you think
> you know is said to your face.

There was a time before her,
so surely there will be an after as well.

> He's such a tired thing.
> Very lazy, occasionally hypocritical,
> and entirely too stubborn in his ways.
> Oh, but she loves him.

Feeling tired isn't a sin.
Certainly not something
to be ashamed of.

> My mask looks like
> shit today.

OPEN LETTER #32

Dear—,

I've never been the type of person that needs help sorting thing out in my own mind. No matter how utterly dreary my writing can get sometimes. I have volatile, self-deprecating moods, and I learned long ago that alone time can do wonders for the soul. For my soul.

For me, it's a necessity. I need periods of utter silence to function. Tranquility in the morning for my first cup of coffee, more calm in the night when I just want to sit, listen to music, and forget about the rest of the world. Independent to a fault. So unuse to living with others that that's how I've become. I adore you for trying to break through the transparent bubble around me and going out of your way to find a place for yourself, but you've brought a hammer and all that surrounds me is soap. It pops easily. And you do it so abruptly that it startles me away.

People are always different. I'm not the type that will suddenly decide to help you tear down my defenses if you keep approaching me with constant callousness. Do you know how astoundingly difficult it is to find the will to do things when the world is talking over my thoughts? When the safety net I surrounded myself with is *forced* to grow to fit someone else?

I don't need any more voices vying for my attention. Rest assured, I'll call you when I do. Respect that I need to sort things out in my head, that I need time to prepare myself on my own because my mind doesn't take kindly to the unsolicited.

I am perfectly willing to let you in. But at my own pace. I promise not to take too long. I'm not such a failure of a man to keep someone waiting to the point of doubt, of restlessness, of irritation.

For now, tact, my dear.

Tact.

Beautiful

She has scars birthed from cruelty,

but they're made beautiful

by how proudly she wears them.

NOTE TO SELF

Distance is terrible.

Even worse if the two of you were never actually together in the first place. So, stop being an idiot. Those endorphins will fade. Stop trying, stop wanting for something more. Don't push your feelings onto someone that's only available to talk when they're bored.

That person—yes, that one smiling in your head—knows what they want, and they'll go after what they want as well. Take the hint and back off. You live more than ten thousand miles away. You can't compete with someone that sits right beside them. You can't compete with someone they do want to be with, so stop trying already.

Chased love isn't love… it's just unhealthy. And you need to stop planning your future around someone who doesn't plan you in theirs. You're a friend, always have been. Nothing more, everything less.

Accept it, mope for a few nights, un-pause life.

Stop this now.

NOISE

Too much exists in my mind,
A cacophony of different voices, a chorus of farewells,
Echoes of regret that fight for a place,
As if I'm not thinking of them every single day,

They keep me up at night, and I'm tired of the noise,
I miss silence, I miss solace, I miss poise,
But I'm stuck with these images; I'm prisoner to these words,
Fighting for dominance that I've long curbed,

The world is alive, slipping past, trickling away
And time, that cruel friend, doesn't bother teaching me how to play,
He leaves me here, alone with my manic,
Where I'm going deaf and sanity escapes—laughably tragic,

These voices are wearing me down now, my head feels full,
So I'll lay it down for a while,
I'll sleep and hope and pray,
That I'll be better fit to deal with them the next day.

Instead

I know it's okay to show frailty.
To bear that tender spot I hide
somewhere deep in my marrow—
you'll accept it.
As you always have.
But, if given the choice…
I'd rather you see me strong.

Finally

No more alcohol to drown my sorrows. No more food to escape the bitter taste of regret that settles like bile on my tongue.

Perhaps... that's for the best.

Because there's no peace to be found at the bottom of a bottle, and I've drowned my senses too long already. My senses have clouded over, and I've forgotten that there's always solace to be found in wreckage, kindness during ages of uncertainty, and most of all, love, when we feel none at all.

So, it's enough now.

It's enough.

Everything's always the same. Just made worse with a hangover.

Sometimes we just need to unlearn how to hope for more.

It's okay if you don't return my sentiments.
(I won't love you any less.)
It's okay if you don't see that I'm trying.
(I won't force you to.)
I will never hold my feelings against you.
(They're not your fault.)

Waiting,

Waiting,

Always waiting.

PART IV

Recovery

*"Find your light,
and revel in it."*

Time passes.

The sun will continue to rise, and with it, the jagged edges of your heart will wear themselves down, and you'll be safe from the stinging cuts of errant memories running rampant inside of your mind.

So, brave this now, treasure up the pain, and find whatever lessons might lie in them. Because it does get better. Those struggles will guide you through the rest of your life. Allow them to be gentle reminders of how easy it is to find a reason to laugh in this dark world—and how it should never be so hard.

OPEN LETTER #27

Dear —,

You speak such pretty words and do far too many things. You've always loved hard. Too serious for your own good. That isn't criticism. I'm glad you care for things so delicately. But it's no wonder that when you found out about my feelings, you thought I wanted the same affection you offered to so many others. The ones you thought were right—maybe they were. But I didn't want that. Because that isn't us, and I don't want to be stuck in the same category as the very ones I helped you get.

I'm quite happy on my own. Returned feelings would be nice, though I'm past the point of hoping. I like what we have. I wouldn't trade it for the world. I simply want what I've always wanted. The one thing I desire from all those I allow close enough to damage me.

Happiness. Peace. Contentment.

I want it all for you.

Bring a chair to this world I have the pleasure of calling mine. Smile and laugh at inside jokes that are too old and too stupid to still be laughed about. If you'd like, bring someone that you believe makes you shine your brightest. I wouldn't mind. Truly. Just sit by my side, as you've done for the past how many years. Why do things need to change? The only adoration I expect from you is the sort you've been giving me all since the beginning. So, allow me to offer you the same.

Because I still know you hate the cold. Because I know you're favorite tunes and the kind of expression you make when you've found something wonderful and cheap to eat. Because I still and will always have a lot of love to give. Much more than I know what to do with.

So, let me love you until eternity ends and the world begins again.

It isn't as difficult as you make it out to be.

Devotion

And so, she offers me her heart.

Open and bright and entirely without price.

I can feel the slivers of old cowardice race up my back, trying to command me—it succeeds in contorting my face. I know this. Because I have to physically fight against the downward struggle of skin and sinew, trying not to scare her.

But every doubt, every passing fear is silenced when she's still there. Eyes huge and unblinking, waiting for something I don't know how to give.

But I will try.

For her.

What You Make Of It

Life's always a little wrecked. Its edges creased. Sentences halted midway. More than a few pages torn, and some singed right to the spine.

But will you really let that stop you from finishing it?

Cure

And though it's against everything I can remember, I reach out, trying to find light in a world I already know is too dark to offer me anything.

I sit and wait and—hope.

Because that's the only cure for the rotting brew of bitterness twisting my gut.

I...

Upturned lips and crinkled eyes,
Echoes of bliss and warm goodbyes.
So, how good am I hiding this?

SECRETS OF THE SELF

Surround yourself with people who know you, who love and care for you. Show them your face, allow them to accept you for who you are at your base, and I promise that you will want for nothing.

Ruminating has always reminded me to accept. But now I know that those same horrid thoughts of my past kills all my hopes for my future.

Write about what hurts. Write about your fears. Your insecurities. Your passions. The page will never judge you.

And ink—accepts.

The world will never become darker from your smile, so do it often, do it freely, and most of all, do it without restraint.

Be bold. Be cynical. Be unforgiving. Be apologetic. Be you. But when all is said and done, and you find yourself with a pile of regrets and too many mistakes—because yes, try as you might, this will happen. Be the one that learns from them.

Haven

Stay wrapped here in my arms where space between us doesn't exist and sighs are drowned by the press of ribs against ribs.

I'll show you comfort so real that the rest of the world will become nothing more than a bad dream.

Me

It's hard for me to speak.

Hard to put into words

the gladness that lights your eyes

at the sight of me.

Me.

Not some shallow,

stainless reflection of me

without flaws.

Daybreak

Darkness bends when I open my eyes.

Slides and curls and twists,

Slinking into corners

where it can strive and fester.

It constantly struggles.

Trying to keep itself alive,

but there's no point.

Shadow will always recede

in the face of light.

Be Proud

Stand up.
Lift your chin.
And walk beside me.
I don't need another shadow.
Only you.

It Takes Two

You keep asking me to pick you up,
but I'm already staggering under the weight
of my own burdens.
I can't carry yours, too.
But if you find the will to walk with me,
then I wouldn't mind pushing you forward
every now and again.

Wraith

I see you often.

In an empty lot.

A crowded room.

In your messages.

And the smile that lights

my face when I do

makes life worth living.

New World

I once dreaded her smiles like the approach of a square world's edge, and yet, here I stand now—of my own volition, wanting for nothing more than the courage to make those lips tilt, widen, and brighten my sky.

Realize

It's time I forgave.
Not only you, but myself.
There's no reason for me
to keep picking off the scabs
of my own abuse.

You cared for me when I didn't think I was worth caring for

Thank you for that.

My confidence
is my own.

I won't let your
leaving take that
away from me.
Not again.

Grin

Infectious laughter makes me hurt.
Don't give me that face.
I meant my cheeks, silly.
I'm happy, too—sometimes.
Your presence keeps me so.

Peace

I want to explain, but I don't always say it right.

How do I convey the million, buzzing bees inside of my head, arguing in sharp, wistful tones about a thousand and one dilemmas—

When they fade into a quiet hum whenever you say my name?

Mango

Trying to stand, to focus my gaze, to command the rippling heat in my chest as it attempts to crush me with a coil of joy, sorrow, and intense relief now that I have you in my arms.

OPEN LETTER #29

Dear—,

I'm here once again. Not lost and lonely. Not tired either. No exhaustion from the turbulence of the world moving along around me—I'm in that place. That happy one I thought existed only beyond my dreams and in other people's lives. Because I didn't know heaven could be on an uncomfortable cloth seat with bad lighting and shit music playing in the background. I didn't realize that the noise of other people could be so soothing, and I certainly didn't think I'd actually come to one day enjoy the cold.

But here, hopefully not just this once, I learned the true meaning of recovery. I basked in the glory of being so filled with happiness that the word brimming seemed inadequate. Of feeling so entirely loved and accepted that my flaws and all my insecurities suddenly didn't matter—perhaps they never did.

Everyone deserves to be loved, they say, though not everyone will have the privilege. There were days I thought I wouldn't have it either. Weeks when I wholeheartedly believed no one would ever see me the way I fantasized in my head. Months of pure nothing. But for reasons beyond comprehension, your presence quieted every single voice, every thought. Until even that doubting monster in the back of my mind was eased into a state of... well, not peace, but something that felt a lot like it.

During the early hours of January second, when the rest of the world was still drunk out of their minds and motionless in bed, sleeping off the final dregs of another year. We stopped by that overpriced airport store to buy what must've been our fifth bottle of water while we waited for whatever accident (boon) responsible for the flight delay passed, and when you fell asleep on my lap, I couldn't hold in my adoration.

You were just so... comfortable. Content. Almost to the point of offense, really. Between the easy lines of your face and the exhaustion that curved my shoulders downward, I wonder why all I could do was smile. Very stupidly at that. The world just seemed so beautiful then. I knew it was because of you. Your quiet breaths were the only thing that mattered. From the steady rise and fall of your chest to every minor twitch, I memorized it all. It was so easy to focus. The weight on my shoulders didn't feel quite as heavy. Or perhaps it was because I had a reason to stand a little straighter... yes, I like that explanation. I'll go with that.

Oh, I adore you. Thank you. Thank you. Thank you.

Solitude

When the world is cold,
And the nights are lonely,
I sit. I drink. I write.
And I become my own best friend.

Sundown

During that infinite moment,
before the stars break,
and the world is lit aflame,
I find the beauty in goodbye.

SCRAWLS

I never loved the sound
of my name as much as I do
whenever it leaves your lips.

> I've been lost a while.
> Tired and hungry, too.
> Thank you for finding me.

Happiness is fleeting?
So is pain, and sadness,
and everything else.
Now, go out and change that.

> Allow me to remain
> by your side.
> Just for a little while.

SCRAWLS

> And only when she falls silent
> with her music,
> do I see the appeal in letting
> time slip away.

Around you,
my volatile mood tempers itself,
and I find myself closing my eyes
in something that feels a lot like peace.

> Sometimes, even the weather mocks you.
> Never let it bring you down.

Build a callous on your soul
and you won't have to worry
about what they want you to be.

> My soul will never be denied.

Serenity

Breathe.

Truly breathe.

Deep enough to gather

a few more pieces of yourself.

Slowly now.

One.

Two.

Three.

Move

You are happiness.

That much is clear.

So, what am I waiting for?

Sky

I regret my weakness.
The young, hesitant desire that
unleashes the coward in my bones.
But not you. Never you.
How could I ever regret the one
shaft of light
that shines upon this harsh world,
reminding me that somewhere beyond—
there is a sky.
And it's bright enough to illuminate
every shadow in my way.

Revelations

I saw it in her eyes when she blinked up at me, tapping her finger on the cherry wooden tabletop, utterly uncaring for the ringing of the kettle that signaled the start of the new day–

She loved me. She adored me. Beyond conscious reason. Beyond any and all doubt. Every layer I'd shown and each she had yet to see.

And I knew...

Life would never be the same.

Healing

I never knew my soul so starved.

Where every whisper of my name feels like a blessing. Where each brush is a balm against aged calluses. Where every press of lips feels like shafts of light seeping into the cracks under my skin, gluing the broken pieces back together and showing me that there is no poison inside. No rot.

Only bruises.

Blossoming yellow and healing.

Unyielding

Bleeding knots in my stomach,
coiling harsher and tighter,
urging me to break.
There are some things, however,
that cannot be done.
Things I will never allow.

Listen

I don't have much to offer,

Even less to give,

But if you'll allow me the privilege

of your thoughts,

Then these bandages I so often carry,

May help mend your soul.

SPRINT

Sighs slip past lips,
 syllables tangled over themselves
like weary limbs.
Sweat bleeds through pores,
encompassing webs of fire and heat
that warm, but never burn.
Not truly.
Heartbeats stagger and race,
competing for something beyond,
lost in the unknowable distance—
past the infant dawn,
just over the bend.
And though it hurts to run,
though these lungs
have already endured too much…
Still, I carry on.
Despite not knowing what awaits me
over the horizon.
Because pain and hardship changes a man.
But love changes him, too.

Stop

He runs from the weight he carries,
fast and far, overburdened and weary.
Always trying to escape.
He's so caught in his own mind
that he forgets that the past
is little more than a thin chain
with imagined manacles
and self-conjured weight
that never fails to run with him.
It's time he realized that this
whatever it is, whatever it may be—
It's enough now.

Dawn

Fledgling smile on my face,
Clinking iron lifted from my chest,
And, before me, the open road,
Glittering with fresh dewdrops,
And smelling startlingly like the sun,
I'm finally awake.

Choice

Now and always,
I choose to laugh.
I choose to love.
I choose to see joy.
My soul has been
buried long enough.

I love to love.
It's warm and tastes
of things long forgotten.

www.ingramcontent.com/pod-product-compliance
Lightning Source LLC
Chambersburg PA
CBHW070606010526
44118CB00012B/1458